Entity within

Yellow blossoms blooming through generations.

Copyrighted, written, and illustrated by Kristy Winter 2021.

Table of Contents

Table of Contents

Table of Contents

Dedicated memories

By Richard Winter

Love can be a danger

create a rage- mental fear and hate

it can take away your reason- Logic and Common Sense.

Love may build you up and break your heart

it may confuse you and make you unworkable.

Your body may refuse to eat- have cold sweats

chills and fever or make you hot- build your desire as an animal to attach or create passion in another.

Love like water needs control and can become

all things that water can- like clean and dirty

-small and big-slow and fast-

shallow and deep as well as fake.

This is written by my dad to add onto another one of my poems. I added a title and made sure he got the credit for his poem. The rest of the poems are mine.

Essence

Fluffy gentleness

soothes the air.

Streams of light

cleanse this room.

Spirits guard and protect

this space

night and day.

This poem is dedicated to Sasami Conway who has taught me a lot about who I can be.

Daughters

Twin warriors

    Yin and yang

        Hot and cold

Dreamers

    Loving with all their heart.

        Peacemakers

Nature's protectors.

This poem is dedicated to Megumi and Yue who have helped me be the more, I need to be.

Peel

Squirting

juicy

round

mouth watering

tongue tasting

sweet smelling fruit.

Smooth to the touch

air filled pores.

White gelatinous stems

strung together inside

a soft shell,

with a green star on top.

Laid back

Yawning, wiping eyes, closing darkness,

soft soothing calming music,

muscles relaxing, tension relieving,

drifting off................

Happy thoughts, peaceful dreaming,

snoring.

Release

Relax the mind,

slow the heart beat,

breathe deep.

Circulate the rhythm of breathing.

Focus the eyes,

release the tension.

Relax the mind,

slow the heart beat.

Breathe deep.........

Exhale fully...........

Circulate the rhythm.

Focus,

release the tension.

Clear the mind of negative thoughts.

The flash

The short wooden stick is grasped

by the hand and itched against

a brown surface which causes

it to ignite and take flight

to a white, bright, blue light.

Which then travels

to the calling,

of the cylinder wax,

with a tiny string reaching,

for the essence of the light

wanting, urging, to be touched.

The lighted strong stick jumps

toward the string and together

they become strong and bright.

They are tall and one.

For one slight movement

and the stick is drawn away and blown

by a frightful gasp of wind and cries goodbye,

and extinguishes itself.

The waxed cylinder is now

left to brighten the next or be extinguished the same.

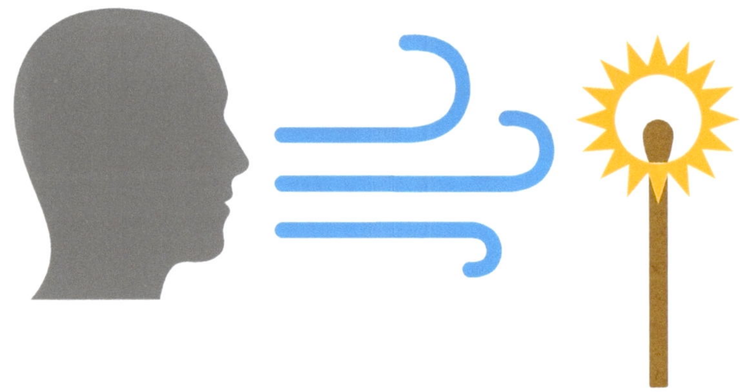

The flash II

It flickers and takes flight

to the dance of the three nights.

It jumps, spins, and flickers

into my little light of my heart

that beats through the night.

One twitch, one itch

with a flick of my finger

it jump starts on until

a wind blows out its bright, red, orange, white,

blue light and says good night.

Eleven twenty

The flame that lights the path

to destruction or har-mon-y.

It burns tall and bright

flickering in the night

past my eye.

It shimmers and shines

in a clear

array of dome-shaped sparkles.

It stays contained

and reaches upward

and shimmies

its way out of the see-through cage.

Whispers

It flickers,

it sways,

it draws me in.

It reflects,

smecks,

and mocks me.

It shines

and taunts me.

Furthermore,

to its degree

to succeed

in following me.

What a bother

I itch, I scratch, it attacks. 

I jump, I scream, "Get off of me!!"

It says, "Ha ha, he he, not me. 

For I am here, don't you see."

I itch,

I scratch,

it attacks. 

What pain,

what endless

sleep I dream 

for only a moment of peace,

please for me.

"Not you, no way,"

they say. "Not today."

Tonight

My eyes are heavy and I can't sleep.

For who is it, but me.

Aah, sniff,

who you see awake,

with eyes so heavy and droopy.

The cement that my eyes wear will not go away.

I yawn and close my eyes,

nothing shall make me sleep but me.

I lay my head down,

try to shut the piercing eyes

that droop so low, aah wipe.

I'll try

here I go.

The night

The sounds I hear are soft and calm.

The banging of the door.

The wind whooshing in my ear.

The soft soothing music.

The train that toots and passes by

as I listen closely from afar.

The light is bright near me and strong to behold.

I lay in bed waiting for my unrelenting sleep.

Will it come? I don't know,

But I hope so.

A far away land

The time ticks by as I shift my eyes

toward the time.

I can't resist

the movement of my eyes flinging

toward the cylinder piece.

I look away once more,

but my eyes

trickle slowly

back toward the one-eyed piece

with figures that ache to change.

How can I stop this unrelenting scene.

The room

The music's pumpin' and bumpin'.

Sounds of air are inhaled and exhaled.

Boom! Bang bang!

Swift soft movements are brought about.

Dancing and prancing come forth.

The SCREEching noise interrupts

the sacred motions.

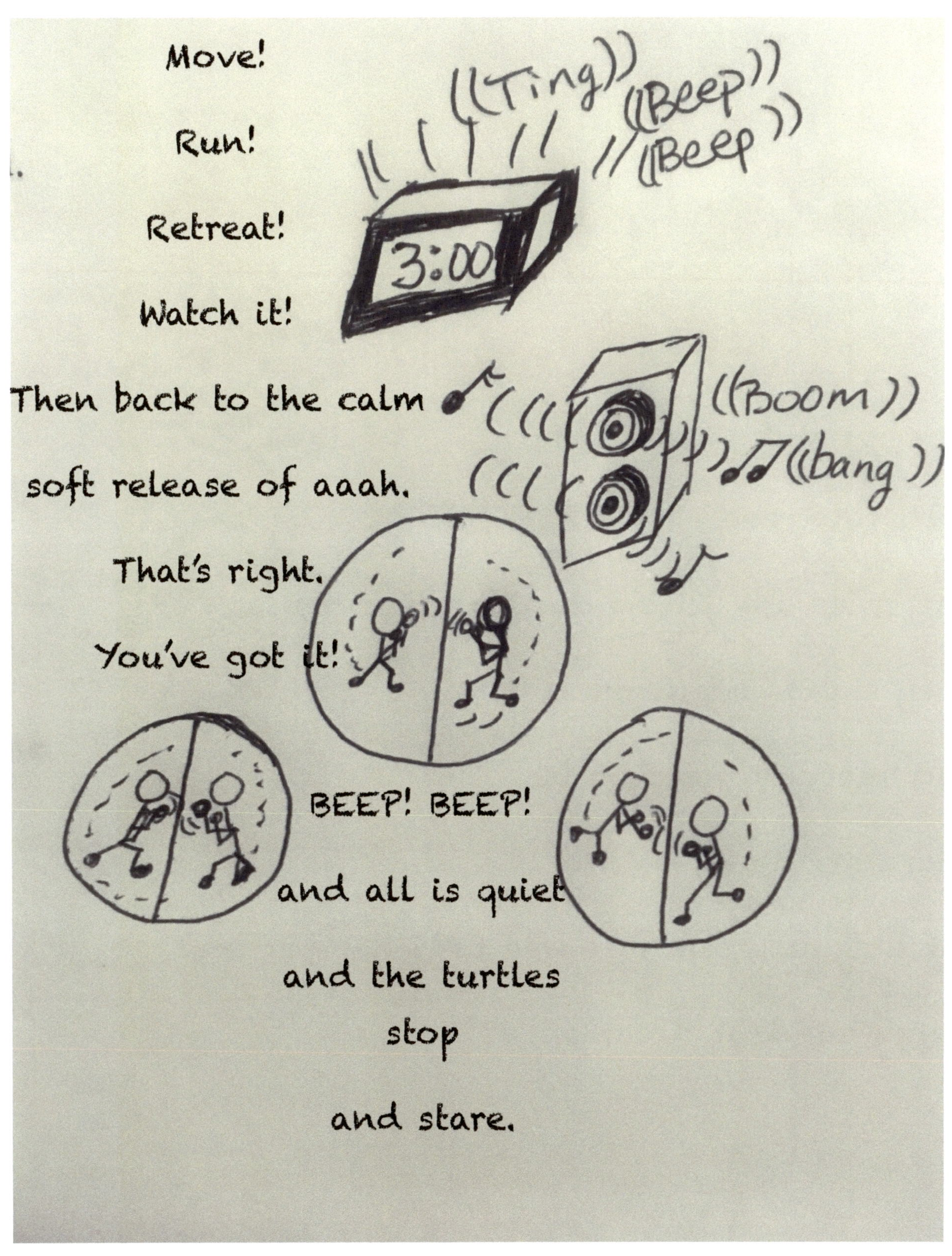

This poem is dedicated to my Kung Fu teacher Dwane Lewis II.

Pictures drawn by Kristy Winter 2021.

The eye

In my mind I see

colorful trees.

The trees are yellow and purple.

They stand out in mind

and feed my need to be.

There are many colors,

but they all seem to come together for me

in my mind of dreams.

Energy

The colorful branches reach

to the sky almost

touching the clouds.

The trunk is sunk

deep within the Earth

almost touching

the spot

where all is centered.

Both ends reaching

to connect

and complete

the oneness cycle.

The point

The beat that hurts,

the sting that trembles into the heart.

The aching pain I have inside.

Why is it here?

Why won't it go away?

Trembling, shaking all around.

It takes my heart.

It stomps, tears, and crumbles it more.

The pain, the ache. No more!

Beat gets faster.

Veins get bigger.

How much more?

I beg and plead, it still persists.

How much more can I absorb?

The space place

Bump pa, bum, bum, bum.

The noise shook the floor.

My feet began to tap,

bounce,

and prance.

My body suddenly wiggled and giggled

to the dance.

I turned and swayed

as the spirit

took forth from the drum beating.

Bum pa, da, bum, bum bum.

Sweep

Screech!

Slam!

Tap, tap, tap, tap, tap, tap,

tap.

Clickety clack.

Clickety clack. Clickety clack.

Swoosh!

Boom rumpa! Rumpa! Rumpa, rampa.

Bump! Bump! Bump! Bum, bum.

Splash! Crash!

Ping!

Ting, ting, ting!

Boom!!!

Beep

Shhhhh.

Tip toe, tip toe.

Tickle, tickle, tickle.

Ha ha, hee hee

Heah, heah, heah.

Tick, tick, tickle, tickle, tickle.

Ha ha, ha ha, ha ha ha.

Ha, ha, aaaah, ha ha!!

Tsssss……,

Ooooops.

The high of life

Eyes brighten, corners of the mouth arise.

The mouth opens wide.

Trickles of laughter come about with a ha ha, ha ha

and a hee hee, hee.

The noise increases.

The heart starts pumping.

The body starts to lose control.

The stomach aches

and the person falls over

with a ha ha, ha ha.

Hee hee, hee hee.

The rolling of the body begins

and the laughter cannot be stopped.

Jump roping

Thump, thump.

Whoosh, whip, snap!

Thump, thump.

The wrists take control.

Whoosh, whip!

The knees bend and the feet
jump one at a time.

Snap! Thump, thump.

Droplets of water run down
the face and body.

Whoosh!

Whip!

Snap!

Thump, thump.

Whoosh, whip, snap!

Thump.

Rain

Wind whistles

in my ear

and little droplets

splash on my face.

The white smoke

comes out from my nose

as I breathe out into the misty air.

My feet begin to jump

and pump in a motion

that is unheard to the normal ear.

As I take flight on the stepping stones of air.

Swept away

Wet beading driplets on my head,

beads of dreams that touch

my soul bringing forth

the child in me.

It takes control and makes me soar,

skipping and hopping to the beat.

The beads dribble down my body

causing me to be free.

I sing, I dance, I prance with the wonderful

beat from the beads

as they take me away

to the world of no fear

but spinning,

jumping dreams.

Spheres

I see splashes

of domed droplets

that dribble and seep in my ears.

They wiggle and swiggle

toward the never ending

canal of my ear.

They swish and sway

all day

as I suck them up

with my portable

container of air.

A life

The prints upon my hand hold strong.

           They are left every time

          anywhere and everywhere.

Their patterns are unique and unified.

      They circle and loop

      round and round

          In a never ending string.

           They jump and sway

            on me here and there

but, never leave my finger no matter

how many times they are printed.

         They are a never ending ink

          passed here and there.

Jailed by freedom

It is strung from here to there

in a never ending process.

Its shape is any way you like

from container to container

but, usually flows in a gravitational manner.

    When

        dropping

            from high heights it swishes

                and pushes its way back

                  to the ground.

It rushes and swirls and hurls to a point

of no return.

Then dries up when it gets burned up

by the monstrous heat of the circling hour.

Dream tears

Blue bird sitting in the tree looking at me.

What do you see in me?

Blue bird, blue bird

I see in your eyes many things.

Calmness, beauty, and a free spirit.

Blue bird what do you see in me?

I see an aching heart of endless dreams.

I see beauty.

I see worry and trembling.

What is it child that you do not see in me?

You do not see the tree,

the roots, the energy.

Look, look deep within me and you will see what is inside you.

Be calm, be trusting, most of all love yourself.

Sound of fire

The animal in you

takes shape and transforms,

the body

into animal form.

The teeth extend

out of the mouth.

The fingers cripple backwards into claws

and the back arches upward.

The beast is formed and is set free,

to run about and fly forward on the ground.

The beast is light as a feather, gravity is no more.

The eyes focus into shape to see

distances far and wide.

Running

Flight of a bird,

speed of a cheetah.

Energy that spreads far and wide

and takes flight

to an enormous

string span of energy lights.

One engine

Electricity

blue static

fingers itching, twitching to the blue light.

Magic fibers between

the small hands.

Magnetic streams

becoming bigger.

Blazing blue light is coming

from within

and pushing out.

Mind gets clearer.

Past becomes future,

future becomes present,

present becomes past.

Sense of time

Rooted deep within the core of the hard soil,

a spirit lies.

She posses an energy that could shake

the universe with one thought.

She is a healer of the soul.

One look and you are in a trance.

She steps into your mind

and heals your emotional core.

Electricity in motion,

breathing life into all your cells

and bringing you home

inside yourself.

Healed and free

you breathe and awaken.

Finally at peace,

rooted and deep.

Centered and strong.

Bright and flowing

as you send her and all you know,

your loving hugs.

She thanks you

and sends you love back.

Minds

Spinning,

twisting

spheres.

Orange,

blue,

red spheres.

Green spirals

spinning out of control.

Pitch black darkness.

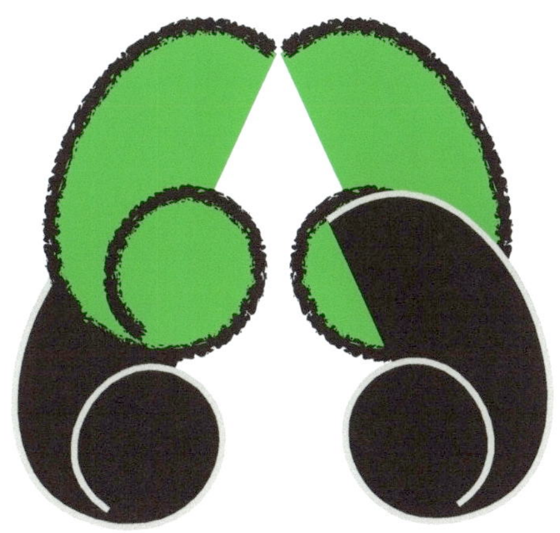

The way

Thundering pulse

whipping streams

of masquerade.

Beaming lights from above.

Smashing palms.

Cracking bones.

Intense eyes

of streams of gold.

Blood lines pumping.

Leaves blowing.

Flutes tooting.

Screaming, yelling.

Heart beat slowing.

Pulse jumping, at peace.

Lights of passion

Wide stances, long legs stretching to the sky.

Joints p

o

p

p

ing,

muscles tightening and relaxing.

Movements from

left   to   right,

forward

and back.

Kicks and punches are thrown and dodged.

A screech shakes the audience

and silence becomes the teacher.

Beats of gold

Mystic dreams catch the eye and set you free.

Spaces to behold and stories untold.

Special sites to see that drop into one's ear.

Visions of the eye from forgotten pasts,

play an important role.

Streams of pearly whites

and wavy lines

take my breath away

for a moment in time.

The words are spoken and tears are shed

from here to there.

But, one short breath takes hold

of my frigid heart and opens it wide

and warms it inside.

Vision

Ancient circles upon the face

tell many stories.

These stories are within

the beads worn around the neck.

They are the symbols

upon the body that resonate sacredness.

Protection

The sword of light is drawn

from its sheltered container,

and zipped from side to side.

A glimmer of blue light

resonates from its blade.

The blue blazing light

swivels and spins through the darkness.

Bringing forth a spectacle

of light,

to shatter

the dark presence

that night.

This poem is dedicated to Larry Conway. A man of honor and love who has taught me a lot about my inner self. Thank you.

The beyond

The eyes that see

deep within the soul.

They open the thoughts

to the mind.

Only the spirit warrior

will let you through the gates.

The human form

ascends

and asks the spirit warrior to show

the secrets unknown.

The warrior will answer

or ignore depending on whether the spirit warrior

believes the human form is ready to see

this new form.

Spirit warrior

The eternal light

of hope, peace, and love,

gives you the strength

to go on

and be fearless.

Calmness with oneness channels,

the positive peace chi for each battle.

Its job is simple.

To cleanse the mind,

body,

and spirit to be whole.

When the negative weakling comes,

the positive overcomes,

conquers, and defeats it.

Signals from the heart

The double edged sword.

Which way does one see it?

One side is dark and the other light.

Which do you pick?

I pick the light but, am drawn to the dark.

I gather my strength, energy, and root into the Earth.

I walk toward the light

and bow my head in forgiveness.

The light has me stand.

You are loved.

My body is filled with a bright white blue light

that cleanses me from

all darkness, worry, and dread.

I am finally at peace and smile.

Sensual spirit

The soul is cleansed

and the pain gone.

It is time

to start anew

and live true

to one's self.

Be full of light

and live the life

you've hoped for

many years.

Savor, the moments and spread the cheer

of love throughout the new year to come.

Feel free, feel loved,

and feel the peace forevermore.

A thought

Beauty is said to be in the eyes of the beholder.

It is compared by many women here and there.

A look in the mirror tells the beauty of the unknown.

Outer beauty can be found anywhere,

but inner beauty is what is special.

Breathe deep the eternal love within.

It is there if you dare

to open your eyes and see within.

Smile and share your inner beauty.

Next time look deep within not out

for inner beauty goes beyond the years

as outer beauty fades.

In closing of this book, I want to give a special thanks to my Kung Fu teacher Dwane F. Lewis II for encouraging me to write this poetry book. I also, want to thank Larry Conway, Sasami, Megumi, and Yue for all their opinions of my designs in this book and their loving support. Another person I want to thank is Amy Web, my creative writing teacher at Emporia State University, for helping me to improve my poetry skills. Finally, I want to thank my parents for their support and encouragement.

I love poetry and writing, because it helps me release my inner passion and express who I am. Writing poetry has helped me through all of my emotional experiences and battles. The more poems I write the better I feel. As a little girl I always wrote songs and stories outside with Mother Earth. The trees and animals always calmed me and inspired me. I hope you enjoy these poems. One thing that I've learned about poetry is it doesn't have to rhyme and you can have the freedom to write it however you want.